1

NAVIGATING ThE STAFF ENGINEER'S PATH: A COMPREHENSIVE GUIDE TO TECHNICAL LEADERSHIP AND CAREER ADVANCEMENT

Contents

Forward

In the steadily developing scene of innovation, the job of a Staff Specialist has become progressively urgent. As associations endeavor to enhance and adjust, they require old pros who can mix profound specialized mastery with powerful administration abilities. This guide expects to enlighten the complex excursion of a Staff Designer, offering bits of knowledge, procedures, and reasonable exhortation to explore the difficulties and immediately jump all over the chances intrinsic in this persuasive position.

The Development of the Staff Specialist Job

The Staff Designer job has advanced altogether throughout the long term, rising above conventional limits of unadulterated specialized capability. Previously, specialized greatness alone may have gotten the job done, however the present mind boggling and dynamic workplaces request a more extensive range of abilities. Staff Designers are not just expected to succeed in their specialized spaces yet additionally to lead, guide, and drive development inside their groups.

Figuring out the Center Liabilities

At the core of the Staff Specialist job lies a mix of specialized dominance and initiative artfulness. The core duties of Staff Engineers will be broken down in this guide, including mentoring and technical leadership, navigating the complex decision-making web, and influencing organizational outcomes. We will investigate how Staff Specialists add to structural plan, guaranteeing the adaptability and heartiness of frameworks through compelling audits and vital preparation.

The Difficult exercise: Specialized Abilities and Initiative

A Staff Designer's process is portrayed by the sensitive harmony between keeping up with profound specialized abilities and developing successful initiative capacities. We will dig into the fundamental specialized skills that recognize Staff Architects, incorporating remaining current with innovation patterns, active coding, and adding to framework plan. At the same time, we will investigate the delicate abilities imperative for progress, like correspondence, coordinated effort, compromise, and the capacity to understand people on a deeper level.

Making a Lifelong Way

For those trying to navigate the Staff Designer's way, defining clear vocation objectives is vital. This guide will give significant experiences into how people can characterize their profession directions, look for and give criticism actually, and take part in persistent figuring out how to remain ahead in a consistently developing tech scene. Exploring the subtleties of profession movement, we will talk about the different achievements and techniques for ascending the stepping stool while making significant commitments to ventures and groups.

Overcoming Obstacles and Developing Resilience The path to

success as a Staff Engineer is not without obstacles. Equivocalness, tension, and group elements can introduce imposing hindrances. These difficulties will be confronted head-on in this guide, which provides practical solutions and strategies for increasing resilience. By investigating genuine situations looked by Staff Architects, we plan to outfit peruses with the apparatuses to explore hardships while staying under control and concentration.

Gaining for a fact: Contextual analyses and Models

Hypothetical information frequently finds its actual worth when applied in functional circumstances. This guide will introduce contextual investigations and models drawn from the encounters of prepared Staff Specialists. These true situations will act as important examples, outlining fruitful methodologies, as well as entanglements to stay away from. Readers can gain a deeper understanding of the role's nuanced aspects by learning from others' successes and failures.

Enabling with Assets

In an industry that blossoms with information sharing, we will organize a rich assortment of assets for Staff Specialists. From books and articles to gatherings, letups, and online networks, this guide will give a complete rundown of source for nonstop learning and systems administration. By utilizing these assets, Staff Architects can remain at the cutting edge of innovative progressions and interface with similar experts.

Conclusion: Navigating the Future As this brief introduction to the role of the Staff Engineer comes to an end, we will begin an investigation of the many facets that make up this dynamic position. Whether you are an old pro holding back nothing a maturing engineer trying to climb the positions, this guide is intended to be your sidekick in exploring the complicated, testing, and tremendously remunerating scene of the Staff Specialist's excursion. Go along with us as we disentangle the layers of specialized administration, profession advancement, and self-improvement that characterize this compelling job in the always developing universe of innovation.

Key Liabilities of a Staff Designer

1. Technical Management:

At the center of a Staff Specialist's liabilities lies the capacity to give specialized initiative. This includes having profound specialized ability as well as actually directing and impacting the group towards effective results. Staffs Architects are supposed to set specialized course, go with informed choices, and move trust in their colleagues through their capability and vital vision.

2. Mentorship and Training:

Staff Specialists assume a urgent part in tutoring and training less experienced colleagues. This includes sharing information, giving direction on accepted procedures, and cultivating a climate where nonstop learning is energized. Staff engineers contribute not only to their own personal development but also to the organization's overall success by investing in the development of their team.

3. Joint effort and Correspondence:

Powerful cooperation and correspondence are principal for Staff Architects. They need to overcome any barrier among specialized and non-specialized partners, making an interpretation of intricate ideas into reasonable experiences. Clear correspondence guarantees that all interested parties, from colleagues to chiefs, is in total agreement in regards to project objectives, timetables, and specialized prerequisites.

4. Independent direction and Impact:

Staff engineers frequently take the lead in the decision-making process. Whether it's picking a specific innovation stack, settling on design choices, or settling specialized difficulties, they should explore through intricacies and pursue choices that line up with both transient objectives and long haul procedures. Also, the capacity to impact others, both inside and outside their group, is pivotal for carrying out their specialized vision.

5. Engineering Plan and Audit:

Staff Specialists are depended with the obligation of planning and auditing framework models. This includes surveying versatility, dependability, and execution contemplations. They effectively partake in engineering conversations, propose enhancements, and guarantee that the general framework configuration lines up with the association's goals. Regular architecture reviews contribute to the upkeep of the systems they overseer's health and sustainability.

6. Profound Specialized Ability:

An essential obligation of Staff Specialists is to keep an elevated degree of specialized skill in their space. This includes keeping up to date with industry patterns, figuring out arising innovations, and ceaselessly overhauling their abilities. This profound specialized information not just fills in as the establishment for successful navigation yet additionally lays out their believability among friends and subordinates.

7. Coding and development by doing:

In spite of some positions of authority, Staff Specialists are supposed to hold active contribution in coding and improvement exercises. This not just permits them to remain associated with the specialized parts of tasks yet in addition sets a model for the group. By contributing straightforwardly to codebases, Staff Designers exhibit best practices, code quality, and proficiency, cultivating a culture of greatness inside the improvement group.

8. Framework Plan and Documentation:

Notwithstanding active coding, Staff Specialists are answerable for framework plan and documentation. Documentation that serves as a comprehensive reference for the architecture, design choices, and essential components of the systems they oversee is created and maintained by them. This documentation is pivotal for information sharing, on boarding new colleagues, and guaranteeing the drawn out practicality of the product.

9. Vital Preparation and Road mapping:

Staff Designers take part in essential wanting to adjust specialized drives to more extensive hierarchical objectives. Contributing to roadmaps, outlining technical milestones, and anticipating challenges are all part of this. By having an essential viewpoint, Staff Specialists assist with directing the development of innovation inside their space, guaranteeing that it lines up with the organization's general business methodology.

10. Continuous Adaptation and Learning:

The quickly advancing nature of innovation requires that Staff Specialists embrace persistent learning and transformation. Remaining inquisitive, investigating new devices and approaches, and being available to change are pivotal parts of this obligation. By staying up with mechanical headways, Staff Designers position themselves and their groups for outcome in the always changing scene of the tech business.

In rundown, the critical obligations of a Staff Designer envelop a mix of specialized ability, authority keenness, and a pledge to consistent improvement. Not only is it necessary to strike a balance between these responsibilities in order to meet the immediate technical requirements of the team, but it is also necessary to foster a culture of innovation and excellence within the organization.

Specialized Abilities and Information

1. Profound Specialized Ability:

Staff Designers are supposed to have a profound and far reaching comprehension of the innovations pertinent to their space. This aptitude reaches out past simple commonality, requiring a top to bottom information on systems, dialects, and devices. Their capability ought to envelop both the central components of their field and the most recent progressions, permitting them to successfully go with informed choices and guide their group.

2. Remaining Current with Innovation Patterns:

Staff engineers must keep up with the latest tech industry trends and developments in order to be effective in their jobs. This includes constant picking up, going to gatherings, taking part in online courses, and effectively captivating with the more extensive specialized local area. Monitoring arising advancements guarantees that Staff Specialists can present creative arrangements and remain in front of expected difficulties.

3. Coding and development by doing:

While authority obligations are unmistakable, Staff Designers are as yet involved supporters of the codebase. They effectively participate in coding and advancement exercises, exhibiting best practices and filling in as good examples for the group. This down to earth inclusion keeps up with specialized capability as well as cultivates a more profound comprehension of the difficulties looked by the improvement group.

4. Framework Plan and Design:

Staff Specialists assume a crucial part in planning and architecting frameworks. This includes making versatile, dependable, and productive models that line up with authoritative targets. Capability in framework configuration permits Staff Architects to come to informed conclusions about innovation stacks, reconciliations, and generally framework structure. Routinely looking into and refining building plans guarantees that frameworks develop to fulfill evolving needs.

5. Execution Streamlining:

Understanding the complexities of execution enhancement is pivotal for Staff Designers. This ability includes distinguishing bottlenecks, upgrading code, and improving framework execution. Staff Designers ought to be capable at utilizing profiling apparatuses, investigating asset use, and carrying out improvements to guarantee that product frameworks meet severe execution prerequisites.

6. Security Mindfulness:

In a time of expanding digital dangers, Staff Designers should have serious areas of strength for an of safety best practices. This incorporates information on secure coding standards, encryption systems, and normal weaknesses. Coordinating security into the advancement cycle is fundamental, and Staff Architects ought to effectively partake in code surveys and security reviews to guarantee the power of the product they administer.

7. Information base Plan and Improvement:

Powerful data set plan and improvement are basic specialized abilities for Staff Architects. They ought to know how to choose the right database technologies, create effective database schemas, and optimize queries for performance. This aptitude guarantees that information capacity and recovery processes line up with the general proficiency and versatility objectives of the framework.

8. Continuous Integration/Continuous Deployment, or CI/CD, and DevOps:

Staff Designers work together intimately with DevOps groups to smooth out advancement work processes. Information on CI/Cd practices, mechanized testing, and arrangement pipelines is fundamental. This works with the fast and solid conveyance of programming refreshes, limiting free time and guaranteeing a consistent improvement process.

9. Cloud Technology:

As associations progressively move to cloud conditions, Staff Designers ought to be know about distributed computing stages and administrations. This incorporates grasping framework as code, overseeing cloud assets proficiently, and enhancing costs. Staff Engineers are able to make well-informed decisions regarding the deployment and scaling of applications when they are proficient in cloud technologies.

10. Critical thinking and Investigating:

Proficient critical thinking and investigating abilities are essential for Staff Architects. They ought to have the option to dissect complex issues, analyze issues, and execute viable arrangements. This range of abilities is important in keeping up with framework unwavering quality and tending to difficulties that emerge during advancement and tasks.

In outline, the specialized abilities and information expected for Staff Designers envelop an expansive range of mastery, going from profound specialized capability to remaining current with industry patterns. Offsetting involved coding with compositional plan and improvement, alongside a pledge to ceaseless learning, empowers Staff Specialists to really explore the consistently changing scene of innovation.

Delicate Abilities and Initiative

1. Powerful Correspondence:

Staff Architects should succeed in correspondence to pass complex specialized ideas on to different crowds, including both specialized and non-specialized partners. Clear and brief correspondence cultivates figuring out, arrangement, and coordinated effort inside the group and across the association. Effective meetings, ideas presentations, and ensuring that everyone is on the same page regarding project goals and milestones all require this ability.

2. Group Coordinated effort:

Joint effort is a foundation of progress for Staff Designers. They work intimately with cross-utilitarian groups, cultivating a climate of receptiveness and collaboration. Being congenial and open to assorted viewpoints urges colleagues to contribute their thoughts, prompting creative arrangements. Staff Designers ought to effectively look for input from colleagues and advance a cooperative culture that values aggregate skill.

3. Compromise:

Conflict resolution is a necessary component of leadership. Staff Designers ought to be skilled at distinguishing and tending to clashes inside the group instantly. This includes undivided attention, understanding varying perspectives, and tracking down agreeable arrangements. By cultivating a positive group dynamic and tending to clashes helpfully, Staff Designers add to a better and more useful workplace.

4. The capacity to appreciate people on a deeper level:

The capacity to appreciate individuals on a profound level is significant for compelling initiative. Staff Designers should be receptive to their own feelings and those of their colleagues. This ability helps in grasping group elements, overseeing pressure, and feeling for the difficulties colleagues might confront. By developing ability to understand people on a profound level, Staff Specialists can construct more grounded associations with their groups and upgrade generally speaking camaraderie.

5. Building and Driving High-Performing Groups:

Staff Specialists assume a crucial part in group improvement. They are liable for establishing a climate that supports elite execution. This includes encouraging a culture of trust, giving productive criticism, perceiving accomplishments, and enabling colleagues. Staff engineers make a contribution to the development and achievement of their teams by inspiring leadership and establishing high standards.

6. Navigation and Hazard the executives:

Viable direction is a key initiative expertise. Staff engineers must take into account the technical and business implications when making decisions in a timely manner. This implies evaluating gambles, gauging choices, and imparting choices straightforwardly. The capacity to go with choices certainly, even despite vulnerability, is basic for directing the group and guaranteeing project achievement.

7. Versatility and Adaptability:

Flexibility is essential in the ever-evolving technological environment. Staff Designers ought to be adaptable and open to change, embracing new techniques and changing systems depending on the situation. Leaders who are adaptable are better able to deal with shifting project requirements, shifting priorities, and unexpected obstacles.

8. Using time effectively and Prioritization:

Effective time management is required to manage multiple responsibilities. Staff Specialists should focus on undertakings, assign assets effectively, and set practical courses of events. This ability is significant for guaranteeing that both specialized and administration obligations are met without compromising the nature of work.

9. Mentorship and Training:

Past specialized direction, Staff Designers are answerable for tutoring and instructing colleagues. This includes giving profession direction, assisting people with fostering their abilities, and encouraging a culture of nonstop learning. By putting resources into the expert development of their group, Staff Specialists add to the general outcome of the association.

10. Vital Reasoning:

Vital reasoning includes adjusting specialized drives to more extensive hierarchical objectives. Staff engineers ought to have a strategic perspective and comprehend how their work contributes to the long-term vision of the company. Decisions that not only address immediate technical difficulties but also position the team and the organization for future success require this ability.

In outline, the delicate abilities and administration characteristics of Staff Architects are just about as pivotal as their specialized skill. By dominating viable correspondence, cooperation, the capacity to understand people on a deeper level, and vital reasoning, Staff Specialists can establish a positive and useful workplace, driving both individual and group achievement.

Calling Improvement for Staff Engineers

1. Advancing Clear Calling Targets:

Productive employment improvement begins with spreading out clear and achievable goals. Staff Architects should seize the opportunity to define their career objectives, which may include reaching higher levels of specialized skill, ascending to influential positions, or contributing to specific projects. These goals go about as an aide for capable turn of events and improvement.

2. Searching for and Giving Analysis:

Criticism is a valuable resource for growth. Staff engineers ought to actively seek feedback from teammates, managers, and other team members in order to comprehend their strengths and areas for improvement. Meanwhile, they should give useful analysis to their partners, empowering a culture of predictable improvement and normal assistance.

3. Relentless Obtaining and Capacity Improvement:

The tech business is dynamic, requiring Staff Modelers to stay up with the latest with creating propels. Interminable learning, through courses, declarations, and self-study, is crucial. To stay at the forefront of their field, Staff Architects should identify areas for skill development that are aligned with their career goals and the requirements of the organization.

4. Investigating Calling Development:

Calling development incorporates prevailing in one's continuous occupation as well as expecting the ensuing stages. To grasp the association's assumptions for professional success, staff specialists ought to effectively draw in with their chiefs. This could remember taking for additional commitments, driving key drives, or acquiring new capacities to prepare for additional raised level positions.

5. Building a Specialist Association:

Getting sorted out is a basic piece of employment improvement. Staff Experts should successfully participate in industry events, gatherings, and online organizations to build a specialist association. Open doors for information sharing, mentorship, and, surprisingly, potential professional success are given by interfacing companions, pioneers, and tutors.

6. Making the most of Chances to Lead:

While particular significance is an indication of the Staff Originator work, embracing drive open entryways is essential for calling improvement. This could be doing driving jobs, giving younger coworkers advice, or taking part in dynamic cycles effectively. Staff engineers who obtain initiative abilities are ready for more extensive obligations and expanded hierarchical impact.

7. Upgrading Scopes of capacities:

Staff designers ought to contemplate growing their ranges of abilities to stay versatile and flexible. This could remember gaining ability for new programming lingos, examining different areas of advancement, or securing data in related spaces. Expanding positions Staff Architects as significant resources for the organization and improves the capacity to add to various projects.

8. Investigating Various leveled Culture:

For professional success, it is fundamental to grasp the authoritative culture and explore it. The qualities that Staff Architects hold ought to be in accordance with the mission, vision, and culture of the association. This incorporates observing association components, collaborating truly with accomplices, and contributing decidedly to the overall work environment.

9. Changing Specific and Organization Capacities:

Finding a balance between specialized expertise and initiative skills is frequently a part of Staff Designers' career development. Discovering some sort of agreement ensures that Staff Experts can contribute truly to both the particular and key pieces of their positions.

10. Building a Singular Brand:

A strong individual brand can basically impact livelihood improvement. Staff Planners should successfully display their dominance through responsibilities to open-source projects, creating particular sites, or talking at get-togethers. Building a singular brand spreads out authenticity inside the business as well as opens up open entryways for composed exertion, mentorship, and expert achievement.

All things considered, calling improvement for Staff Experts incorporates a proactive method for managing objective setting, incessant learning, drive development, and imperative frameworks organization. By assuming a sense of ownership with capable turn of events and staying delicate to industry designs, Staff Engineers can investigate their livelihood ways really and contribute conclusively to their affiliations.

Difficulties and Arrangements

1. Adjusting Specialized and Initiative Obligations:

Challenge: Staff Architects frequently face the test of adjusting their profound specialized liabilities with the requests of influential positions. Striking the right harmony between involved specialized commitments and initiative can challenge.

Solution: Lay out clear assumptions with the group and association about the harmony among specialized and initiative obligations. Delegate undertakings properly, encourage cooperation inside the group, and focus on powerful using time productively to guarantee the two angles are tended to.

2. Managing Uncertainty:

Challenge: Staff engineers may encounter situations where ambiguity prevails because the technology industry is inherently dynamic. Indistinct undertaking prerequisites, developing innovations, or moving hierarchical needs can present difficulties.

Solution: Accept that the industry is full of ambiguity. Foster critical thinking abilities, discuss straightforwardly with the group to explain vulnerabilities, and lay out a culture that energizes flexibility. Nimble techniques and iterative methodologies can be important in exploring uncertain circumstances.

3. Dealing with Strain and Stress:

Challenge: The requests of specialized initiative, project cutoff times, and hierarchical assumptions can prompt elevated degrees of stress for Staff Architects. Adapting to pressure is pivotal for keeping up with efficiency and prosperity.

Solution: Execute pressure the executive's strategies, like laying out sensible objectives, focusing on undertakings, and rehearsing care. Empower a strong group culture that perceives and addresses individual and aggregate stressors. Normal breaks and a sound balance between serious and fun activities add to long haul versatility.

4. Tending to Group Elements:

Challenge: Conflicts between teammates, diverse personalities, and varying levels of expertise can all complicate team dynamics. Exploring these elements to keep a strong and high-performing group is a typical test.

Solution: Encourage open correspondence inside the group, make a culture of shared regard, and address clashes proactively. Empower group building exercises and put resources into group advancement programs. Show others how its done, exhibiting positive way of behaving and joint effort to establish the vibe for the group.

5. Profession Movement and Acknowledgment:

Challenge: Staff Designers might confront difficulties with regards to vocation movement and acknowledgment for their commitments. This could result from an absence of clear headway open doors, restricted deceivability of accomplishments, or hierarchical designs that don't sufficiently perceive specialized skill.

Solution: Participate in straightforward conversations with the executives about vocation objectives and assumptions. Look for criticism routinely to comprehend regions for development and ways of exhibiting influence. Advocate for an organized vocation movement structure that perceives specialized greatness and initiative commitments.

6. Changing Organizational Structures:

Challenge: Associations go through changes, for example, rebuilds, consolidations, or changes in innovation stacks, which can present difficulties for Staff Designers in adjusting to new designs, cycles, or devices.

Solution: Remain informed about hierarchical changes, discuss straightforwardly with the group, and look for lucidity on what changes mean for current tasks and obligations. Show versatility by effectively captivating in learning new apparatuses or techniques, and work together with the group to all in all explore advances.

7. Scaling Specialized Impact:

Challenge: As Staff Designers progress in their vocations, scaling their specialized impact to influence bigger tasks or the whole association can be a test.

Solution: Make an effort to actively seek out opportunities to impart knowledge, contribute to architectural decision-making, and instruct junior team members. Stakeholders should be clearly informed about the technical vision and its significance to the organization. Team up with different pioneers to adjust specialized methodologies to more extensive business objectives.

8. Keeping up with Balance between serious and fun activities:

Challenge: The requesting idea of specialized influential positions can make it trying to keep a solid balance between fun and serious activities.

Solution: Lay out limits among work and individual life. Delegate assignments really to stay balanced, and urge the group to focus on prosperity. Associations can uphold balance between serious and fun activities through adaptable plans for getting work done, remote work choices, and drives advancing representative prosperity.

9. Supporting Variety and Consideration:

Challenge: Staff engineers may face difficulties in building and leading diverse and inclusive teams, particularly in male-dominated fields.

Solution: Effectively advance variety and consideration drives inside the group. Encourage a comprehensive culture where all colleagues feel esteemed and heard. In the process of decision-making, promote a variety of points of view and actively address any biases that might emerge.

10. Aligning Organizational Objectives with Technical Vision:

Challenge: Staff Designers might confront hardships in adjusting their specialized vision to the more extensive hierarchical objectives, prompting a likely misalignment between specialized choices and business goals.

Solution: Participate in customary correspondence with key partners to grasp hierarchical objectives. Obviously well-spoken the specialized vision with regards to these objectives, underscoring the effect on business results. Cultivate joint effort with different offices to guarantee specialized choices add to by and large authoritative achievement.

In rundown, tending to difficulties requires a blend of compelling correspondence, proactive critical thinking, and a pledge to constant improvement. Staff Designers who effectively look for arrangements and encourage a positive group culture contribute not exclusively to their self-improvement yet additionally to the outcome of their groups and associations.

Examples and Case Studies

1. Engineering Redesign at TechCo:

Challenge: TechCo, a quickly developing tech organization, confronted versatility issues with its current framework engineering. The Staff Designer, Sarah, drove an extensive engineering update to address execution bottlenecks and oblige the rising client base.

Solution: Sarah started a series of architectural reviews with teams from across the organization to get ideas and feedback. She proposed a particular and versatile microservices engineering, carrying out changes steadily to limit disturbances. The outcome was a profoundly versatile framework that settled current presentation issues as well as situated TechCo for future development.

2. Spry Change at Programming Developments:

Challenge: Programming Developments, a fair sized programming improvement organization, battled with a sluggish and inflexible advancement process. John, a Staff Designer, perceived the requirement for a coordinated change to improve productivity and responsiveness.

Solution: John advocated the reception of lithe systems, presenting Scrum practices and stressing persistent combination. He coordinated team-training workshops and worked with management to establish an agile-friendly culture. The outcome was a more versatile and cooperative improvement process, bringing about quicker conveyance of great programming.

3. Flexibility during High-Traffic Occasions at Online business Goliath:

Challenge: A web based business goliath confronted difficulties during top traffic occasions, encountering site blackouts and slow reaction times. Mary, a Staff Specialist, was entrusted with improving framework flexibility to deal with high traffic loads.

Solution: Mary executed load testing to recognize bottlenecks and flimsy spots in the framework. In order to deal with sudden spikes in traffic, she introduced auto-scaling mechanisms and enhanced caching strategies. Through careful testing and checking, Mary guaranteed the framework stayed strong during appeal periods, bringing about better client experience and expanded income.

4.   StartupHub's   Mentorship Program Implementation:

Challenge: StartupHub, a startup hatchery, coming up short on organized mentorship program for its designing groups. Alex, a Staff Designer, perceived the requirement for mentorship to speed up the expert development of junior specialists.

Solution: Alex started and carried out a mentorship program, matching experienced engineers with junior colleagues. He coordinated standard information sharing meetings and gave assets to ability improvement. The mentorship program worked with information move as well as made a cooperative and strong group culture, adding to the progress of the startup projects.

5. Cloud Relocation at Big business Arrangements:

Challenge: Agility and scalability presented challenges for Enterprise Solutions, a large company with legacy on-premise systems. Chris, a Staff Specialist, drove the drive to move basic frameworks to the cloud.

Solution: Chris fostered a far reaching relocation plan, tending to information security, administrative consistence, and limiting personal time. He worked together with cross-utilitarian groups, guaranteeing a smooth progress to cloud foundation. The effective movement brought about better framework execution, expanded adaptability, and decreased functional expenses for the association.

6. Conflict Resolution in GlobalTech's Cross-Functional Teams:

Challenge: GlobalTech, a worldwide tech organization, experienced clashes inside cross-useful groups because of different working styles and social contrasts. Emily, a Staff Designer, perceived the requirement for compromise to keep up with group union.

Solution: Emily worked with group building studios, stressing open correspondence and figuring out alternate points of view. She executed normal input meetings and made channels for compromise. The end result was a more harmonious and productive workplace where diverse teams effectively contributed to the success of the project.

These contextual analyses represent how Staff Designers have handled different difficulties, exhibiting their initiative, specialized ability, and vital reasoning. Every model underlines the significance of proactive critical thinking, coordinated effort, and the positive effect that Staff Architects can have in their groups and associations.

Assets for Staff Specialists

Books:

"The Supervisor's Way: An Aide for Tech Pioneers Exploring Development and Change" by Camille Fournier

"Group Nerd: A Product Designer's Manual for Cooperating with other people" by Ben Collins-Sussman, Jenny Wanger, and Matthew McCullough

"Roused: Step by step instructions to Make Items Clients Love" by Marty Cagan

"An Exquisite Riddle: Frameworks of Designing Administration" by Will Larson

"The Practical Developer: Your Excursion to Authority" by Dave Thomas and Andy Chase

"High Result The executives" by Andrew S. Forest

"Building Transformative Structures: Support Consistent Change" by Neal Passage, Rebecca Parsons, and Patrick Kua

Articles and Websites:

Rands in Rest - Experiences on authority and the board by Michael Lopp.

The Successful Architect - Articles and assets by Edmond Lau, zeroing in on further developing designing viability.

Stripe's publication Increment covers a wide range of leadership and software development-related topics.

The Lead Engineer - Meeting talks, articles, and assets zeroed in on administration in tech.

ThoughtWorks Experiences - Articles on programming improvement, administration, and innovation patterns.

Meetups and conferences:

The Lead Designer - A gathering devoted to designing initiative.

QCon - A worldwide series of gatherings on programming improvement and design.

DevOpsDays - Occasions overall zeroing in on DevOps practices and culture.

Speed - O'Reilly's meeting on building and keeping up with tough frameworks.

Meetup - Nearby meetups and occasions where you can associate with different experts in your space.

Online Training:

Coursera - Offers seminars on initiative, the executives, and different specialized points.

Pluralsight - An innovation zeroed in learning stage with seminars on programming improvement, administration, and then some.

Courses on technical subjects, project management, and leadership skills are available through LinkedIn Learning.

Udacity - Gives nanodegree programs in regions like programming advancement, information science, and simulated intelligence.

Online People group:

Stack Flood - A people group for developers to ask and respond to specialized inquiries.

Dev.to - A stage for software engineers to share thoughts and interface with the designer local area.

Reddit - r/programming - A subreddit for conversations connected with programming.

The Designing Chief - A Leeway people group for designing directors.

CodeProject - A people group for sharing code tests, articles, and conversations.

These assets cover a great many themes, from specialized abilities to initiative turn of events. Whether you're searching for books, articles, meetings, online courses, or networks, these choices can assist you with remaining informed, foster your abilities, and associate with different experts in the field.

End

All in all, the excursion along the Staff Designer's way is a dynamic and complex investigation of specialized administration, nonstop learning, and profession improvement. This guide has given bits of knowledge into the key liabilities, specialized abilities, and delicate abilities fundamental for flourishing in this powerful job. Staff Designers act as key parts, offsetting profound specialized mastery with viable authority to direct groups and associations toward progress.

From laying out clear profession objectives and embracing mentorship to exploring difficulties and building high-performing groups, the Staff Designer's job requires an all encompassing methodology. The difficulties, as illustrated, present open doors for development, versatility, and advancement. By embracing powerful arrangements, Staff Designers can beat deterrents, adding to a positive work culture and encouraging group achievement.

The contextual analyses and models displayed this present reality utilization of Staff Designers' abilities, showing their effect on ventures, groups, and whole associations. The significance of strategic thinking, adaptability, and productive collaboration in achieving meaningful outcomes is emphasized in these tales.

Moreover, the aide accentuated the meaning of constant learning and remaining informed about industry patterns. The recommended assets, including books, articles, gatherings, and online networks, act as important buddies on the excursion, giving an abundance of information and potential open doors for proficient turn of events.

As Staff Designers explore their vocations, embracing difficulties, leveling up initiative abilities, and keeping a harmony between specialized skill and vital reasoning are critical. Staff engineers' resilience and success as they shape technology's future are aided by the tech community's collective experiences, insights, and support networks.

May this guide motivate and engage Staff Architects to embrace their jobs with energy, explore difficulties with versatility, and keep making effective commitments to the always developing scene of innovation. The path taken by the Staff Engineer is not just a career; it's a constant excursion of development, development, and initiative.